show me the future

TO STEVE,

WITH MY BEST WISHES.

WERNER.

18. 08. 2004

show me the future
engineering and design by werner sobek

Conway Lloyd Morgan

avedition

Einleitung

Wer das Glück hat, im Restaurant Wielandshöhe einen Fenstertisch zu ergattern, wird einzig durch den Anblick von R 128, das wie ein silbern-stählerner Harlekin aus den grauen Anzügen Stuttgarts hervorsticht, von Vincent Klinks Küche abgelenkt. R 128 ist eine Hommage des Architekten und Ingenieurs Werner Sobek an die Stadt, in der er wohnt - und es ist sein Zuhause. Es ist außerdem ein Statement über seine Ideen und Prinzipien in einer lebendigen, realen Umgebung. Im Gegensatz zu den Fertigpalästen, Farnsworth Freeholds und Dymaxion-Domen, die in der Vergangenheit eher architektonische Absichtserklärungen abgaben, ist Sobeks Studie über Umweltverträglichkeit, Materialeinsatz und die Ebenmäßigkeit von Design kein Kabinettstückchen, sondern ein veritables Wohnhaus.

Zwar trifft es zu, dass Werner Sobek seine Fähigkeiten als Ingenieur in seine Arbeit als Architekt einbringt und die Vision des Architekten in die Arbeit des Ingenieur einfließen lässt, aber eine solche Aussage propagiert eine zweifelhafte Dichotomie. Viel eher lässt sich sagen, dass in Sobeks Arbeit die Anforderungen zweier paralleler Disziplinen vereint sind; Präzision wird mit Ästhetik kombiniert, und dabei bleibt der Blick auf Funktionalität und den Kontext gerichtet. Ob es um einen einfachen Seilendbeschlag geht oder um den größten Flughafen der südlichen Hemisphäre, seine Arbeit ist ein Zusammenspiel aus intellektueller Stringenz und visueller Sensibilität.

Und so sollte es bei jeglicher Architektur sein, die diesen Namen verdient. Sobek fügt diesen Qualitäten noch ein feines Gespür für Zweckmäßigkeit hinzu, die auf die ethischen Verpflichtungen eines Gebäudes im aktuellen Kontext ausgerichtet ist: Umweltverträglichkeit, technische Leistungsfähigkeit, innovative Materialien, gesellschaftliche Relevanz. Bei seiner frühen Arbeit mit Frei Otto hat er nicht nur die Leichtigkeit von Materialien kennen gelernt, sondern auch eine gewisse Leichtigkeit in der Ausführung, dank der wir in seiner Arbeit sowohl den Wert als auch das Vergnügen eines minimalen Eingriffs und einer exakten Lösung erkennen.

Werner Sobek studierte nicht nur bei Frei Otto, sondern übernahm später seinen Lehrstuhl als Leiter des Instituts für Leichte Flächentragwerke in Stuttgart. Hier geht es nicht nur um Materialstudien, sondern vor allem um neue Technologien aller Arten, und die Forschung in diesem Bereich wirkt sich auch auf Sobeks Architektur und Ingenieurskunst aus. Neue Konzepte, wie glasfaserverstärktes Glas und adaptive Gebäudehüllen, finden durch seine Arbeit und seine Projekte den Weg aus dem Labor in die Realität. Dabei handelt es sich nicht um technische Kunststückchen um ihrer selbst willen, sondern um einen sorgfältig kalkulierten, interdisziplinären Ansatz zu effizienten und nachhaltigen Lösungen für die Bauwerke der Zukunft. Schaltbare Fenster zum Beispiel lassen sich auf Knopfdruck verdunkeln (oder reagieren auf veränderte Lichtverhältnisse).

Man könnte dies für praktischen Schnickschnack halten, für Hightech-Zauberei. In Sobeks Händen werden solcherlei Elemente aber zu einem selbstverständlichen Bestandteil des erweiterten Potenzials eines Gebäudes. Projekte wie Haus R 129 sind wegweisend für eine Zukunft, in der Gebäude nicht statisch sind, sondern anpassungsfähig und über ihre Struktur hinaus funktional. Diese Funktionalität ist nicht auf das Gebäude beschränkt, sondern richtet sich auf seine menschliche, ökonomische und ökologische Umwelt.

Eine solche zielstrebige Architektur ist nicht in der Gegenwart gefangen, sondern der Zukunft verpflichtet. Das bedeutet für Sobek nicht einfach, die Lebensdauer eines Bauwerks und der darin verwendeten Materialien zu beachten, sondern darüber hinaus zukunftsweisende Projekte zu konzipieren. Es handelt sich also um einen visionären Prozess, der in der Realität wurzelt und von einem Bewusstsein für Farben und Formen genährt wird, das Wissen und Fertigkeiten zur Leidenschaft werden lässt.

Taking a view

Be fortunate enough to get a table by the window in the Wielandshöhe restaurant, and the only distraction from Vincent Klink's cuisine is the sight of R 128, shining like a silver and steel harlequin amid the grey suits of Stuttgart. R 128 is architect and engineer Werner Sobek's homage to the city he lives in: and it is also his home. It is a statement of his ideas and principles, but in a living, real setting. Unlike the plug-in palaces, Farnsworth freeholds and Dymaxion domes that have formed architectural statements of intent in the past, Sobek's study in environmental efficiency, use of materials and design regularity is not a show space but a real place.

To say that Werner Sobek brings the skills of an engineer to his work as an architect and the vision of an architect to his work as an engineer is true, though it perpetuates a discredited dichotomy. Rather one should say that Sobek's work meets the requirements of two parallel disciplines, bringing precision together with aesthetics and taking a perspective on both functionality and context. Whether it is a simple cable shackle or the largest airport in the southern hemisphere, his work shows an intellectual rigour and visual sensitivity combined.

So indeed should all architecture worthy of the name, it might be said. To these qualities Sobek adds a wider sense of purpose, directed to the ethical obligations of building in a modern context: respect for the environment, technical efficiency, material innovation, social relevance. His early work with Frei Otto taught him about lightness of materials, and also a certain lightness of touch, enabling us to appreciate in his work both the value and the pleasure of a minimal intervention and an exact solution.

Werner Sobek not only studied under Frei Otto but later succeeded him as leader of the Institute for Lightweight Studies in Stuttgart. This is a focus for new technologies of all kinds, not just materials studies, and this research flows through into Sobek's architecture and engineering. New concepts such as fibre-reinforced glass and adaptive building envelopes move from the laboratory to the real world through his work and projects. This is not technical wizardry for its own sake, but a carefully directed multi-disciplinary approach to devising efficient and sustainable solutions for the buildings of the future. Switchable windows, for example, can turn from dark to light on demand (or in response to external change).

Some might find this a convenient flourish, a high-tech trick. In Sobek's hands such items become a logical part of the extended potential of a building. Projects such as the R 129 house are signposts to a future in which buildings are not static but adaptive and move beyond structure to functionality. The definition of this functionality is not limited to the building itself but to the human, economic and environmental landscape it is to occupy.

A purposeful architecture of this kind is not tied to the present but obligated to the future. For Sobek this does not mean simply considering the total lifetime of a building and its materials, but, beyond that, creating projects whose potential empowers future users. This is a visionary process that is firmly rooted in reality. And it is informed by a visual awareness of colour and form that turns knowledge and skill into passion.

Inhaltsverzeichnis
Contents

structure

Komplexe Strukturen wie die Glasfassaden des Sony-Center in Berlin, das Tragwerk der neuen Generaldirektion der Deutschen Post AG in Bonn oder auch der Messestand der Audi AG sind nur durch die vielfältigen Möglichkeiten der in den letzten Jahren entwickelten computergestützten Entwurfs- und Berechnungsprogramme sowie durch die enge Zusammenarbeit aller beteiligten Planer möglich. Da das Tragwerk wesentlichen Einfluss auf die Gestalt eines Bauwerks hat, sind bei einer solchen Zusammenarbeit ein Verständnis des Architekten für Fragen der tragenden Konstruktion und ein Verständnis des Ingenieurs für die Intentionen des Entwurfs besonders wichtig. Ein Beispiel für die Ergebnisse einer derartigen engen Zusammenarbeit ist der mit dem Architekten Helmut Jahn geplante New Bangkok International Airport. Dieses Bauvorhaben ist auch gekennzeichnet durch seine vielfältigen Funktionen in Überlagerung mit einer extremen Größe. Dies bedingt Komplexität in der Planung - eine Komplexität, die erst durch klare und einfache Gliederung der Gesamtstruktur eine Reduktion des Erscheinungsbildes auf das Wesentliche erlaubt. Gleiches gilt für die vielfältigen innovativen Sonderkonstruktionen aus Stahl und Glas, die für das Sony-Center in Berlin entwickelt wurden. Diese haben einen wesentlichen Anteil an der Gesamtstruktur und prägen das Erscheinungsbild entscheidend.

Complex structures such as the glass façade of the Sony Center in Berlin, the load-bearing structure of the new headquarters of Deutsche Post AG in Bonn or the exhibition stand of Audi AG, have only been made possible by the numerous facilities offered by the computer-aided design and computation programs developed over recent years as well as by the close co-operation of all planning engineers concerned. Since the load-bearing structure is of crucial importance to the shape of a building, such co-operation calls on the part of the architect for a good understanding of structural problems and on the part of the engineer for a good understanding of the intentions of the design. One example of such close co-operation is the New Bangkok International Airport which was planned in collaboration with the architect Helmut Jahn. This project is also characterised by its numerous and varied functions combined with extreme size. This requires complexity in planning - a complexity which allows the visual appearance to be reduced to the very essential by a clear and simple structuring of the overall construction. The same applies to the various innovative special steel and glass structures developed for the Sony Center in Berlin. They form an essential part of the total structure and have a decisive impact on its appearance.

Werner Sobek

Seilfassade im Sony-Center Berlin
Cable supported façade at Sony Center Berlin

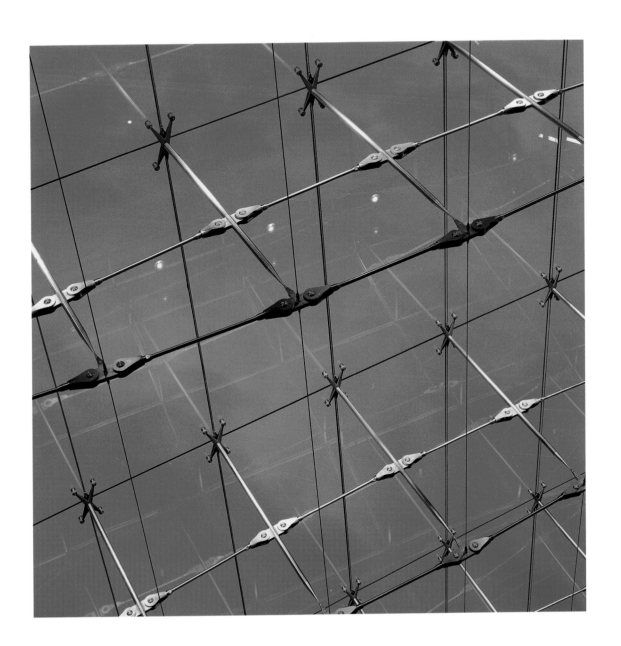

14 Le Corbusier bezeichnete in einem berühmten Zitat das Haus als "Wohnmaschine". Der Ausdruck ist zum Mantra des Modernismus geworden, in dem die Werte der Maschine - Zuverlässigkeit, Funktionalität, Effizienz - denen der Kunst gegenüberstehen. Tatsächlich ist "Kunst" im allgemeinen Sprachgebrauch mit Selbstdarstellung, Dekorativität, innerem Dialog, sogar Freiheit konnotiert, aber in der ursprünglichen Bedeutung hat Kunst mit Können und Fertigkeiten zu tun und ist durch die Kopplung von Kreativität an bestimmte Fähigkeiten definiert. Für die Betrachtung der künstlerischen Qualität von Werner Sobeks Werk ist diese tiefere Bedeutung die wichtige.

Nehmen wir beispielsweise das Haus in Stuttgart, das er für sich und seine Familie als Wohnhaus gebaut hat. Stuttgart ist eine grundsolide, bürgerliche Stadt. Verlässlich, stark, aber nicht protzig - wie ein Mercedes-Benz. In einer solchen Stadt ein Glashaus zu bauen mag auf den ersten Blick lobenswert provokant erscheinen, wie eine Ermutigung der Einwohner zu mehr Extravaganz.

Tatsächlich hat es aber fast den gegenteiligen Effekt, da vor allem die Schlichtheit und Logik der Konstruktion offenbar sind: eine Box mit einer regelmäßigen Fassade aus Glaselementen, eine schlichte Brücke, die den vierten Stock mit dem dahinter liegenden Hang verbindet, und eine Treppe, die das Gebäude auf allen Ebenen im gleichen Winkel durchkreuzt. Aufgrund der Hanglage hat man von hier aus einen herrlichen Blick über die Stadt, aber die Bäume um das Haus und der Hang schirmen das Gebäude vor Blicken aus der Nähe ab.

Das Haus ist zum größten Teil aus vorgefertigten Elementen zusammengesetzt, sodass bei maximaler Rezyklierbarkeit eine kürzere Bauzeit möglich und nur wenig Aufwand für das Fundament erforderlich waren. Durch das Glas

"A machine for living in" is how Le Corbusier famously described a house. The phrase has become a mantra of modernism, in which the values of the machine - regularity, functionality, efficiency - are considered as opposed to those of art. Indeed the everday connotation of "art" centres on self-expresion, decoration, inner dialogue, licence, even. But the deeper meaning of the word links it to skill and discipline, in a definition that binds creativity to ability. In looking for the artistic qualities of Werner Sobek's work it is this deeper meaning that is relevant.

Take for example the house in Stuttgart that he built for his family and himself to live in. Stuttgart is a serious, solidly bourgeois city. Reliable, powerful and not ostentatious like a Mercedes-Benz, in fact. Building a glass house in such a city might seem, at first, to be laudably provocative, an attempt to encourage a little more display among the citizenry.

In fact the effect is almost the opposite, for what is at once apparent is the simplicity and logic of the structure. A box, with regular façades of glass panels and a spare bridge linking the fourth floor to the hillside behind and a stairway cutting through each floor at the same angle. Because of the slope on which it is set, it enjoys a panorama of the city, yet the trees among which it stands and the angle of the slope shelter it from observation at close quarters.

The house was constructed largely from prefabricated units, requiring less time on site, minor foundation work and ensuring maximum recyclability. The glass ensures maximum use of daylight, the heating sytem with the triple glazing and a heat sink in the lowest floor of the building maintains an even temperature all year round. So efficient is the glazing that in winter the exterior glass can be starred with frost while the interior remains warm to the touch! All the

R 128: Blick vom Eingangsbereich her
R 128: view from the entrance side

16 wird das Tageslicht bestmöglich genutzt; das Heizsystem mit Dreifachverglasung und Wärmespeicher im untersten Geschoss sorgen das ganze Jahr über für eine angenehme Innentemperatur. Tatsächlich ist die Verglasung so effizient, dass sich im Winter von außen Eisblumen bilden können, die Scheiben von innen aber handwarm bleiben. Der Strombedarf für das Haus wird - im Jahreszyklus - komplett über die Photovoltaikpaneele auf dem Dach gedeckt. Insofern verkörpert das Haus viele von Werner Sobeks Design-Prinzipien: Vorfertigung, Wirtschaftlichkeit der Mittel, minimaler Energieverbrauch et cetera.

Das Haus ist aber weit mehr als eine Demonstration von Prinzipien oder eine Ideenvitrine. Es ist auf eine unabhängige, skulpturale Weise abstrakt, ähnlich wie die Werke von Don Judd oder Sol LeWitt, in denen der Minimalismus eine lyrische Qualität erhält. Vor allem aber ist es ein Heim, das zum Wohnen gebaut ist, und zwar offensichtlich ein außergewöhnliches. Und dazu sind Häuser schließlich gedacht, wie auch Le Corbusier wusste, denn die oft vergessene Fortsetzung des berühmten Zitats lautet: "Wir brauchen Tageslicht (...), eine geregelte Temperatur, ein gesundes Raumklima und die Schönheit guter Proportionen."

electrical energy required for the energy concept and control engineering is produced by solar cells on the roof of the building. In this way the house literally incorporates many of the principles that are enshrined in Werner Sobek's approach to design: prefabrication, economy of means, minimal energy and so on.

But the house is far more than a statement of principle or a showcase of ideas. It has an independent, sculptural quality of abstraction, like a work by Don Judd or Sol LeWitt, in which minimalism becomes lyrical. And, more importantly again, it is a home, built to be lived in, and by all accounts it is an extraordinary place in which to live. And that is what a house is for, after all: as Le Corbusier knew, for the famous quotation forgottenly continues "we must have sunlight (...), controlled temperature, healthy conditions and the beauty of good proportions."

Innenansicht mit Treppe
Interior view with stairways

Axonometrie des Gebäudes
Axonometric representation of the structure

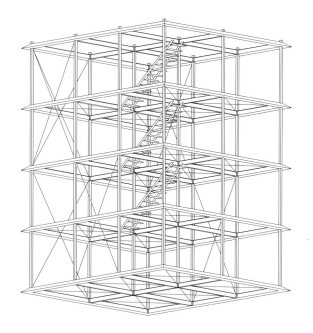

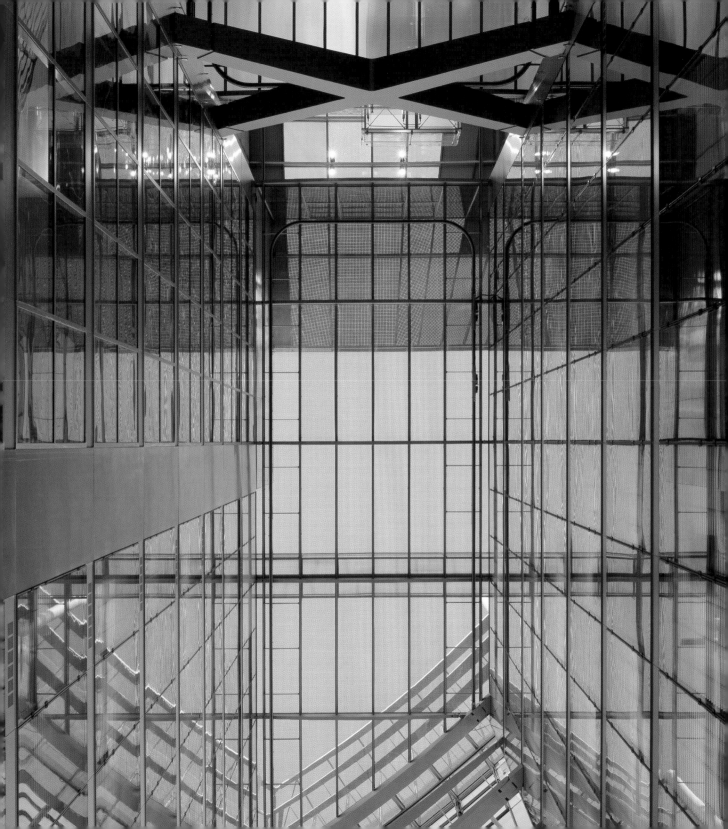

Weightless - New Bangkok International Airport

34 Wie wir alle wissen, ist ein Warren-Träger einfach ein umgedrehter Pratt-Träger, in dem alle Teile sowohl Zug- als auch Druckbelastung aufnehmen können. Das zeigt, dass viele Konstruktionslösungen auf vertikaler Ebene umkehrbar sind. Einfache Erkenntnisse dieser Art können enorme Auswirkungen auf die Gestaltung bestimmter Konstruktionen haben.

Helmut Jahn, der den Wettbewerb für den neuen Flughafen von Bangkok gewann, bat Werner Sobek und sein Team um Unterstützung beim wichtigsten Teil der Gestaltung: den tragenden Konstruktionen und den Fassaden. Jahns Entwurf sah ein einziges Hauptterminal vor, umrahmt von einem System von "Concourses", über die man die Flugzeuge erreicht und die wie zwei liegende Kreuze hinter dem Terminal angeordnet sind. Das Terminalgebäude selbst ist eine vollständig verglaste Box unter einer Dachkonstruktion, die vor Sonne und Regen schützt und über das Terminal hinausreicht, um auch die hinteren Teile der Kreuze zu überdachen. Das Dach, vierzig Meter über dem Boden, sollte so dünn wie möglich sein und aus der Ferne wie eine scharf umrissene, über dem Terminal schwebende Scheibe wirken. Es wird tausend Meter lang und zweihundert Meter breit sein.

Werner Sobek ermöglichte dies dadurch, dass er das Dach über eine Reihe von Trägern laufen lässt, deren Form ihrem inneren Beanspruchungsverlauf angepasst ist. Dies lässt die Dachkonstruktion schwerelos wirken und betont gleichzeitig Form und Größe der Fassade. Das gleiche Konstruktionsprinzip wird auch als Träger für die geschwungenen Concourses eingesetzt, die das Terminal mit den Flugsteigen verbinden. Es ermöglicht breite und hindernisfreie Wege für die Passagiere. Um die Leichtigkeit noch stärker hervorzuheben, werden die Concourses ebenfalls verglast beziehungsweise mit Membranen eingedeckt.

As we all know, a Warren girder is just a Pratt truss with vertical and diagonal struts, in which all the members can take tension as well as compression. That is to say, many engineered solutions are reversible in the vertical plane. Such simple insights may have an enormous impact on the design of certain structures.

Helmut Jahn, who won the competition for the new Bangkok airport, brought Werner Sobek and his team in to help work on the main design, for the terminal building. Helmut Jahn's concept was for a single main terminal building frame by concourses giving access to the aircraft and arranged in plan as two horizontal crosses joining behind the terminal. The terminal building would be a glazed box set below a roof structure that would provide shade and protection from rain, and would project beyond the terminal to cover the descending arms of the crosses. The roof, forty metres above the ground, should be as narrow as possible, and appear from a distance like a single clear edge floating above the terminal. It would be two hundred metres long and one thousand deep.

Werner Sobek realised that by repeating and then reversing the load-bearing strut that provided the main support for the roof, this could be achieved very efficiently, and with a minimum of visual impact for the truss itself, so emphasising the overall shape and scale of the façade. The roof structure would then in effect appear weightless. The same element could also be used to frame the curved concourse structures linking the terminal to the departure gates. It would also allow for a wide and unobstructed span for these important passenger routes. To emphasise the concept of lightness, the concourses would be glazed or covered in fabric respectively. The latter presented key challenges not only in terms of dimensions to be covered, but also in terms of acoustic and ther-

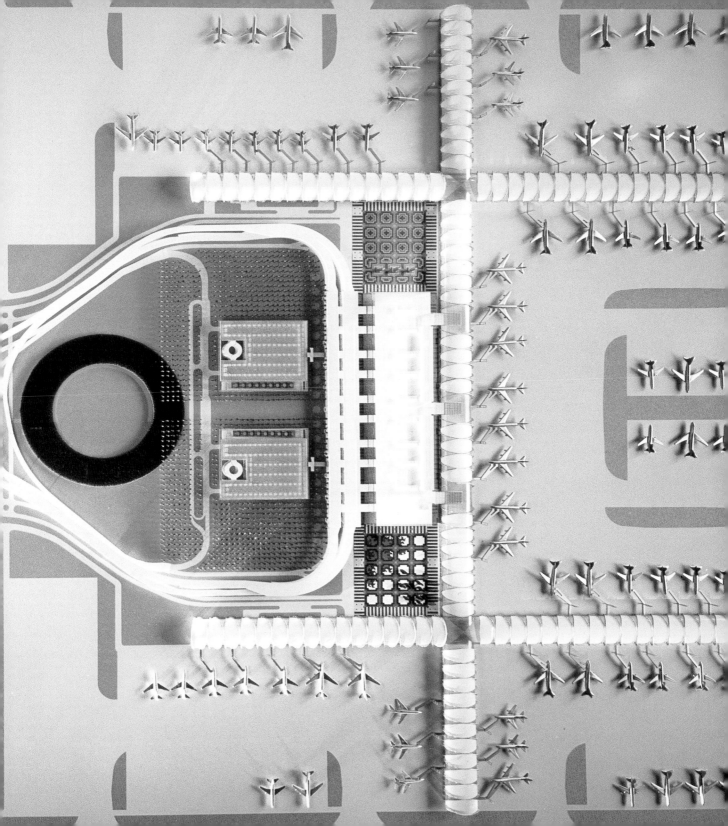

36　Letzteres war eine der großen Herausforderungen, nicht nur wegen der Größe der zu bedeckenden Flächen, sondern auch wegen der akustischen und thermischen Eigenschaften von Membranen, da die Concourses in der Nähe der Start- und Landebahnen und Rollfelder liegen. Die Lösung war eine spezielle Dreifachmembran, die Sobek und die anderen an der Entwicklung beteiligten Partner weltweit patentieren ließen.

Der Bangkok International Airport ist eines der größten Bauprojekte der Welt - schon die Concourses sind zusammen über drei Kilometer lang, und WSI richtete eigens ein Büro in Thailand ein, um die Arbeiten vor Ort betreuen zu können. Es ist ein großer Vertrauensbeweis für die Partnerschaft zwischen Helmut Jahn und Werner Sobek, dass sie bei einem Projekt dieser Größe bereit sind, radikal neue Wege zu gehen.

mal control, given the proximity of the concourses to runways and taxiing areas. This was solved by using a special triple membrane, for which Sobek and the other partners in its development took out a world-wide patent.

The Bangkok International Airport is one of the largest construction projects in the world – there are over three kilometres of concourse alone, and WSI have set up a branch office in Thailand to handle the on-site work. And it is a strong statement of confidence in the partnership between Helmut Jahn and Werner Sobek that on such a major project they were willing to try radical new solutions.

Modell des Terminalgebäudes
Model of terminal

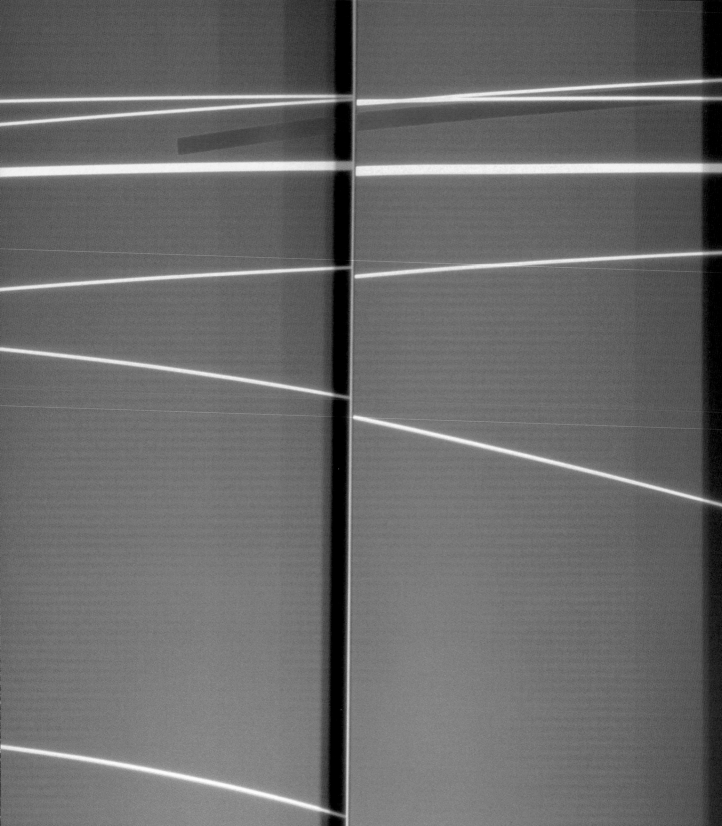

Systems - Mercedes-Benz Exhibition Stand

Der irische Ingenieur Peter Rice zählt sowohl das Opernhaus von Sydney als auch das Centre Pompidou, zwei Ikonen der modernen Architektur, zu seinen Erfolgen. In seinen Memoiren diskutiert er den Unterschied zwischen Architekt und Ingenieur; dabei ist ihm, schreibt er, sehr bewusst, dass er selbst oft als "Architekt-Ingenieur" bezeichnet wurde. Ihm missfällt die darin liegende Implikation, dass die meisten Ingenieure, denen dieser Ritterschlag nicht erteilt wird, automatisch nicht kreativ seien. Er schlägt dagegen als Unterscheidung vor, dass der Architekt erschafft, und der Ingenieur erfindet. Damit meint er, dass die Entscheidungsgrundlage des Architekten eine subjektive, die des Ingenieurs eine objektive ist.

Der Unterschied ist sehr subtil. Zum Teil bekräftigt er die traditionelle Rolle des Ingenieurs, der eher im Schatten des Architekten wandelt als an seiner Seite und damit beschäftigt ist, die Entwürfe des Architekten umzusetzen, statt gemeinsam mit ihm daran zu arbeiten. Diese Ansicht ist jedoch veraltet - schließlich besteht auch ein Generationenunterschied zwischen Rice (1935-1992) und Werner Sobek (1953 geboren). In der Zwischenzeit hat sich der Computer zu einem wesentlichen Werkzeug sowohl des Ingenieurs als auch des Architekten entwickelt; vor allem erlöst er den Ingenieur von den zeitaufwändigen Berechnungen, die so langwierig und unerlässlich waren. Gleichzeitig ermöglicht es der Computer dem Architekten wie dem Ingenieur, in einem Umfeld, in dem in rascher Folge neue Bau- und Oberflächen-materialien auf den Markt kommen, komplexere Formen zu entwickeln. Die Rechenleistung des Computers bedeutet nicht nur, dass notwendige Berechnungen heute sehr viel schneller durch-geführt werden können, sondern auch, dass erstmals eine Annäherung an bestimmte Faktoren, die bislang als unberechenbar galten, möglich wurde. Diese enorme Arbeitserleich-

The Irish engineer Peter Rice, could list both the Sydney Opera House and the Pompidou Centre, two icons of modern architecture, among his many achievements. In his memoirs, he discusses the difference between the architect and the engineer, aware, as he says, that the term 'architect engineer' had often been applied to him, and disliking the implication that most engineers not granted this accolade are therefore unimaginative. As a distinction, he proposes the idea that the architect creates, while the engineer invents. By this he means that the architect uses a subjective process of decision making, the engineer an objective one.

The distinction is a subtle one. In part it invokes the traditional role of the engineer as walking in the architect's shadow rather than at his or her side, and being involved with verifying the architect's proposals rather than working jointly on them. This view might be seen as dated - there is after all a generational difference between Rice (1935-1992) and Werner Sobek (born 1953). And during this time the computer developed to become an essential tool for both engineers and architects, in particular freeing the engineer from time-consuming mathematical calculations, tedious and essential as they were. At the same time, computers empowered both architects and engineers to evolve more complex forms, in an environment in which new materials, both for structural and surface use, were becoming available apace. The ability of the computer to calculate meant not only that previous calculations could be done much more rapidly, but that factors previously incalculable could be closely considered for the first time. This decrease in part of the workload for the engineer and increase in new work led to a more egalitarian relationship between engineer and architect, particularly on complex projects.

Der Stand in Benutzung
Stand system in use

adaptivity

Adaptivität bezeichnet die Fähigkeit eines Systems, sich selbsttätig an veränderte Umweltbedingungen anzupassen. In natürlichen Systemen sind adaptive Prozesse infolge veränderlicher äußerer Einflüsse selbstverständlich. Im Gegensatz zu den natürlichen Systemen sind die aus der Architektur bekannten Systeme statisch - sie reagieren nicht auf Veränderungen ihrer Umwelt, obwohl es eigentlich nahe liegend ist, durch adaptive Prozesse die Funktion dieser technischen Systeme zu verbessern oder ihre Lebensdauer zu erhöhen. In den letzten Jahren hat unser Team wichtige Untersuchungen zum Thema Adaptivität durchgeführt, die eine praktische Anwendung im Bauwesen in greifbare Nähe gerückt haben. Adaptive Gebäudehüllen aus Glas oder Stoff führen zu einer deutlichen Erhöhung des Nutzerkomforts und eröffnen völlig neue Perspektiven für die Gestaltung von Gebäuden. Adaptive Tragwerke ermöglichen es, die Grenzen des Leichten viel weiter hinauszuschieben, als dies mit herkömmlichen Strukturen denkbar ist.

The term "adaptivity" describes the capability of a system to adapt itself automatically to changed environmental conditions. In natural systems adaptive processes caused or triggered by external factors are normal. Unlike natural systems, however, the systems developed by architecture are static - they do not react to changes in their environment although it should be obvious that the function of these technical systems could be improved or their life-span extended by means of adaptive processes. In recent years our team has carried out important studies on the subject of adaptivity, which have brought within reach practical applications of the concept to building construction. Adaptive building envelopes fabricated from glass or textile fabrics considerably increase the comfort of the users and open up completely new perspectives in terms of building design. Adaptive load-bearing structures enable us to extend the limits of lightweight construction much further than could have been thought possible with conventional structures.

Werner Sobek

Métafort in Paris: Modellansicht
Metafort in Paris: view of the model

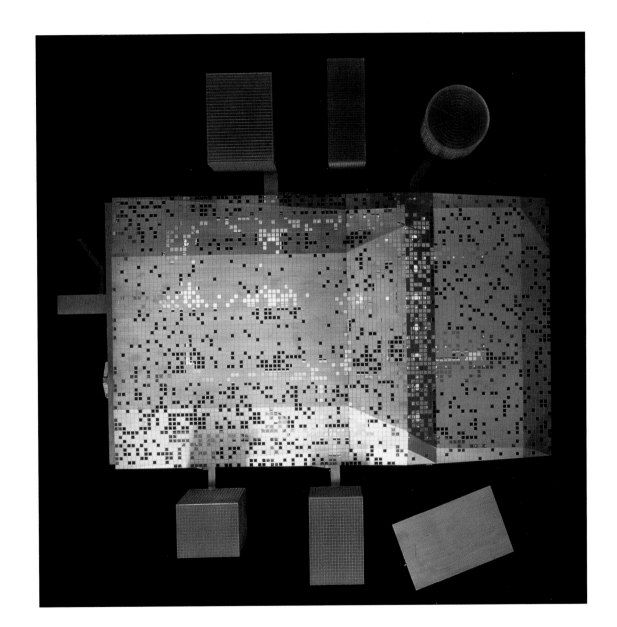

Poetry - Rotating Umbrellas

"Das Problem bei Schirmen", so Werner Sobek, "sind die Speichen. Sie brechen allzu leicht. Warum nicht einen Schirm ohne Speichen bauen?" Und genau das versuchte das Team. Die Idee ist einfach: Der Schirm dreht sich, und durch die Zentrifugalkräfte wird der rund geschnittene Stoff zu einer horizontal rotierenden Scheibe. Allerdings nicht immer: Selbst bei Windstille oszillierte die Scheibe und nahm eine Wellenform ein. Das beeinträchtigte zwar die Wirkung des Objekts als Sonnenschutz keineswegs, aber es war eine Unregelmäßigkeit, und Ingenieure mögen keine Unregelmäßigkeiten. "Wir haben einige Spezialisten für Strömungsdynamik gefragt, die sich das Problem ansahen, es aber weder erklären noch lösen konnten", erzählt Sobek. "Also haben wir selbst weiter experimentiert. Schließlich fanden wir heraus, dass ein Wulst am Rand den Luftstrom gleichmäßiger macht und die Stoffscheibe eben rotieren lässt."

Das Konzept wird jetzt für den Einsatz als Ausstellungsobjekt, für Messen und Ähnliches weiterentwickelt, aber das eigentliche Interesse von Werner Sobek und seinen Kollegen lag in der Grundlagenforschung: "Als wir das Problem schließlich gelöst hatten, habe ich mich sehr gefreut und habe es meinem Sohn abends zu Hause genau erklärt und aufgezeichnet. Er sah sich das eine Weile an und sagte dann: 'Genau wie ein Frisbee.' Und da hatte er Recht."

"The problem with umbrellas," according to Werner Sobek, "is the spokes. They get in the way, and they break. How about a spokeless umbrella?" So the team tried to build one. The concept is simple: the central pole rotates, and centrifugal force lifts the circle of fabric into a spinning horizontal disc. Or not quite: even in still air, the disc oscillated out of the horizontal, rising on one side, then another. This did not necessarily affect the performance of the object as a sunshade. But it was an anomaly, and engineers do not like anomalies. "So we went to see various experts in flow dynamics, who looked at the problem and agreed it was there but couldn't solve it or explain it. So we carried on testing it ourselves. And in the end we found out that if we put a curved lip on the underside of the fabric, that would even up the airflow and keep the disc rotating evenly."

The concept is now being developed for use as a promotional object or for trade fairs and suchlike, but its real interest for Werner Sobek and his colleagues was as a piece of pure research. "When we finally solved the problem, I was very pleased, and that evening at home told my son all about it, drawing out the shape for him. He looked at it for a while and then said,'Yes, it's just like a Frisbee.' And he was quite right!"

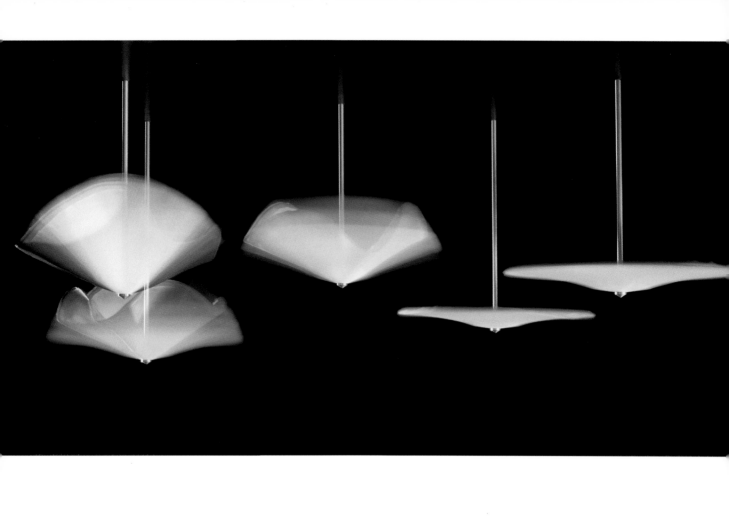

Glas ist aufgrund seiner Transparenz ein besonders faszinierender Baustoff. In den vergangenen Jahren sind seine Einsatzgebiete ständig gewachsen. Ausschlaggebend hierfür waren die Fortschritte, die hinsichtlich der Fragen zum mechanischen Verhalten des Baustoffes, der Krafteinleitung in Glasbauteile und der Entwicklung eines dem Werkstoff angepassten Bemessungsverfahrens erzielt wurden. Gleichzeitig wurden aber auch die Technologien der Glasherstellung, Weiterverarbeitung und Veredlung in erheblichem Umfang weiterentwickelt. Der bewusste Umgang mit den Möglichkeiten nahezu vollkommener Transparenz ist ein prägender Faktor in den Arbeiten unseres Teams.

Because of its transparency glass is a specially fascinating building material. In recent years its applications have been continually expanded. Of crucial importance was the progress achieved in terms of the mechanical behaviour of the material, the transfer of forces into glass components and the development of a dimensioning procedure adapted to the material. At the same time the technologies of glass production and glass processing were considerably developed and enhanced. The conscious handling of the possibilities of almost perfect transparency represents a decisive factor in the work of our team.

Werner Sobek

Nahezu entmaterialisierte Fassade: Kaufhof Chemnitz
Nearly immaterialised façade: Kaufhof Chemnitz

Prototyping - Mercedes-Benz Museum

68

D'Arcy Wentworth Thompsons Buch "Über Wachstum und Form" wird seit 1917 immer wieder aufgelegt, wenn auch mittlerweile in einer gekürzten Fassung. Trotz der Anerkennung seiner stilistischen Eleganz und Originalität hat es eine Weile gedauert, bis seine Botschaft über die mathematische Grundlage natürlicher Formen ihren Platz fand. Heute tauchen in der Architektur mit gegossenen und geschwungenen, der Natur nachempfundenen Formen häufig Modelle aus Flora und Fauna auf. Aber Werner Sobek hält diesen Ansatz nicht für optimal: "Tiere als Modelle für Grundrisse oder dekorative Elemente zu verwenden", erläutert er, "ist nichts für mich. Ich finde es nicht richtig, Tierformen als Grundlage für die Gestaltung einzusetzen. Man muss verstehen, wie natürliche Formen funktionieren, und dieses Wissen kann man auf unterschiedlichste Weise umsetzen."

Der Entwurf für das neue Mercedes-Benz Museum des Architekten Ben van Berkel von UN Studio in Zusammenarbeit mit Werner Sobek als Ingenieur setzt der Marke Mercedes-Benz ein Denkmal. Er sieht eine Doppelhelix vor, die grundlegende biomorphe Struktur, wie Watson und Crick zeigten. Das Gebäude, das in der Aufsicht die Form eines dreiblättrigen Kleeblatts hat, weist von außen eine angenehme visuelle Komplexität auf, während die Helixstruktur im Inneren dem Besucher ermöglicht, sich gleichmäßig durch die verschiedenen Ausstellungsbereiche zu bewegen.

Diese Kontinuität der Besucherbewegung war der Kernpunkt für Architekt und Ingenieur, da sie nicht nur die Kontinuität der Marke Mercedes-Benz symbolisiert, sondern darüber hinaus das Innen und das Außen verbindet: Sichtachsen führen durch den dreieckigen Luftraum in der Mitte in die neun Ebenen des Gebäudes. Der Ingenieur war gefordert, diese Kontinuität in der Verglasung fortzuführen, durch die räumliche Krümmung und die unterschiedlichen Ebenen hindurch.

D'Arcy Wentworth Thompson's book On Growth and Form has remained continuously in print (admittedly today in an abridged edition of the original four volumes) since 1917. For all the accolades the book has had for its stylistic elegance and originality, it has taken some time for its message, about the mathematical basis of natural form, to find its era. Today zoomorphic and biomorphic models are frequent in architecture, using moulded and sinuous forms inspired by the natural world. But for Werner Sobek this is not an ideal approach: "using the shape of an animal as a model for a ground plan or for a decorative form" he explains, "is not an attitude I share. Using animal shapes as a basis for design is not the right way. Understanding how natural forms function, however, that is necessary knowledge, and it can be applied in different ways."

The Mercedes-Benz Museum concept, designed by architect Ben van Berkel of UN Studio, with Werner Sobek as structural engineer, will be a monument to the Mercedes-Benz marque. The design concept is a double helix, perhaps the most fundamental of biomorphic concepts, as Watson and Crick showed. The trefoil form of the building has a satisfying visual complexity from the exterior, while the helical arrangement of the interior allows the visitor to move at an even rate through the various exhibits intended for the building.

The continuity of the visitor's movement through the building was a key concept for architect and engineer, since it not only reflected the continuity of the Mercedes-Benz marque but also linked the interior and exterior, with views, at times, across the building itself, through the central triangular void, into the nine "leaves" making up the building. Part of the engineering challenge was to maintain this continuity in the glazing, through the double curves and changes of level.

Luftansicht des Modells
Aerial view of the model

11

94 Die Welt verdankt Madeleine Vionnet eine ganze Menge: die Pariser Modedesignerin erfand 1922 den Schrägschnitt. Sie entdeckte, dass sich Stoff, der im Winkel von 45 Grad zum Fadenlauf zugeschnitten wird, sehr viel enger um den Körper schmiegt, als das bei gerade geschnittenen Stoffen möglich ist.

Das neue Interbank-Gebäude des Wiener Architekten Hans Hollein in Lima, Peru, hat eine voll verglaste Fassade, vor die der Architekt einen Screen spannen wollte, um den skulpturalen Charakter des Gebäudes zu betonen und Reflexionen zu vermindern: mit dieser Idee kam er auf Werner Sobek zu. Dieser schlug ein Titangerippe auf einem geschwungenen Rahmen mit angewinkeltem oberen Abschluss und parallel zum Gebäude verlaufenden Kanten vor. Ein solches Geflecht wäre relativ transparent und würde kontrastreicher wirken als eine glatte Oberfläche, sowohl aus der Nähe wie auch aus der Ferne. Die parallel verlaufenden Titanrohre sind, wie Madame Vionnets figurumschmeichelnde Kleider, schräg geschnitten und aufgehängt. Die Rohre sind nur an einer Seite verschraubt und an der anderen auf einen Halter aufgeschoben, um so Bewegungen durch Wind und thermische Ausdehnung abfangen zu können. Das Ergebnis ist eine abstrakte, aber sehr natürlich wirkende Skulptur vor Holleins stark gegliedertem Gebäude.

The world owes a great deal to Madeleine Vionnet. She was the Parisian dress designer who in 1922 invented the bias cut. By cutting fabric at a forty-five degree angle to the weave she realised that the fabric would drape the body much more closely, without the straps and padding that had been a feature of earlier, straight-cut designs.

The Viennese architect Hans Hollein's new Interbank building in Lima, Peru, has a fully glazed façade, but the architect wanted to put a screen in front of this to emphasise its sculptural character and to reduce glare: he approached Werner Sobek over the idea. The latter proposed a titanium mesh on a curving frame and with an angled top and parallel side. A mesh would have some transparency and contain more visual contrast, both close to and at a distance, than a single surface. It would also have reduced windage. But a mesh, even in titanium, is flexible, and folds or creases would be unacceptable in the finished surface. So, as with Madame Vionnet's figure-hugging dresses, the mesh is cut and hung at an angle to its rectilinear axes: the top and right-hand edge are fixed, with more flexible attachments along the bottom and left-hand edges to allow for wind movement and thermal expansion. The result is an abstract but very natural sculptural form in front of Hollein's rather formal building.

Die Fassade vom Boden aus
The façade from ground level

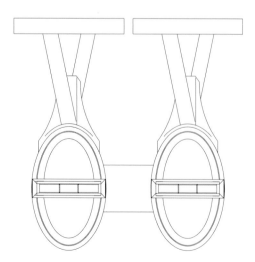

Schematische Darstellung des Befestigungssystems
Diagram of suspension system

Gesamtansicht
General view

design

Nachhaltig überzeugendes Produktdesign zeichnet sich durch verschiedene Kriterien aus. Zu diesen zählen neben der Funktionalität die haptische Qualität, eine innere Logik, eine Erkennbarkeit der Funktion und der Bedienung sowie eine hohe ästhetische Qualität. Diese Eigenschaften gelten aber nicht nur für das Design von Produkten wie Seilendbeschlägen oder Möbeln, sondern lassen sich auch auf andere Bereiche des Gestaltens, etwa im Bauwesen, übertragen. Ein Beispiel hierfür ist die Fußgängerbrücke, die unser Team für die EXPO 2000 in Hannover entwarf. Die vollständig aus Aluminium bestehende Brücke zeichnet sich durch ihre Leichtigkeit, ihre Schlankheit und - dank Vorfertigung - ihre einfache Montierbarkeit aus.

Ein weiteres Beispiel sind die für ein Designmuseum in Essen entworfenen Ausstellungspavillons. Die Hülle dieser Strukturen wird aus seriell vorgefertigten, integralen Wandelementen - so genannten Hardbodies - gebildet. Jede Struktur ist flexibel konfigurierbar und erweiterbar: in der Länge durch den Einbau von zusätzlichen Modulen und in der Breite durch Veränderung der Trägerlängen. Zusätzlich lassen sich einzelne Strukturen von unterschiedlicher Größe über Zwischenelemente koppeln. Die Module der Hardbodies sind multifunktional und enthalten zum einen alle notwendigen Haustechnikanlagen. Zum anderen können sie Eingänge ausbilden oder zur Andockung von externen Standard-Containern dienen. Wie die Fußgängerbrücke zeigt auch dieser Entwurf sowohl in der Formensprache als auch in den verwendeten Materialien große Affinitäten zu anderen Bereichen des Engineering wie zum Beispiel dem Flugzeugbau - und zeichnet sich durch höchste Gestaltungsqualitäten aus.

Convincing product design of lasting quality is characterised by a number of criteria. Among these, apart from functionality and haptic qualities, are an inherent logic, a recognisable function and operation and a high level of aesthetic quality. These characteristics apply, however, not only to the design of products such as cable shackles or furniture but can also be translated into other areas of design such as building construction. One example of this is the footbridge designed by our team for the EXPO 2000 exhibition in Hanover. What makes this all-aluminium bridge special is its light weight, its slenderness and - thanks to pre-fabrication - its easy assembly.

Another example are the exhibition pavilions designed for a design museum in Essen. The envelopes of these structures are formed from batch-produced integral wall elements, so-called hard bodies. Each structure can be flexibly configured and expanded: longitudinally by inserting additional modules and transversally by altering the length of the beams. In addition individual structures of different sizes can be coupled by using intermediate elements. The hard body modules are multi-functional and accommodate all necessary technical equipment. They can also form entrances or be used for docking external standard accommodation containers. Like the footbridge, this design also exhibits, in terms of its forms and materials, a great affinity with other areas of engineering such as aircraft construction and is characterised by the highest level of design quality.

Werner Sobek

Designstudie Zeche Zollverein
Design study Zeche Zollverein

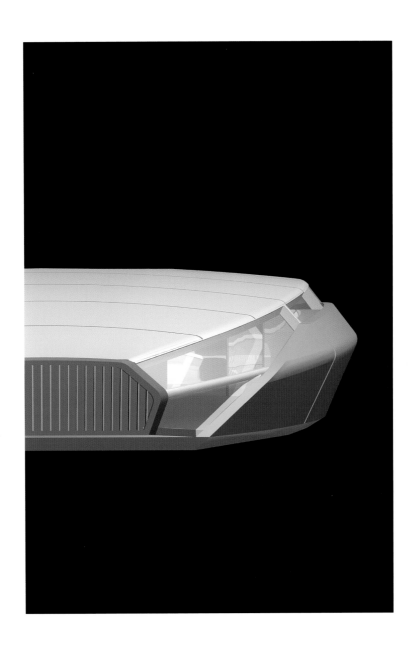

15

122 Die Fußgängerbrücke ist zu einem beliebten Bauwerk der Jahrtausendwende geworden. Von Calatravas Brücke für die Expo in Sevilla über Fosters Millennium Bridge in London bis zu neuen Brücken in Paris, Manchester und anderswo waren solche Projekte im vergangenen Jahrzehnt en vogue. Dies überrascht nicht weiter, wenn man den Brückenbau nicht baugeschichtlich, sondern kulturgeschichtlich betrachtet. Die großen Eisenbahnbrücken des 19. Jahrhunderts in England beispielsweise symbolisieren den Triumph des merkantilen Kapitalismus auf ähnliche Weise, wie die Brooklyn Bridge, die Manhattan mit New Jersey verbindet, als Vorläufer der berühmten Wolkenkratzer, als Ikone der Macht Amerikas gesehen werden kann.

In der ersten Hochphase der Fußgängerbrücke, den 50er Jahren, führten diese Brücken zumeist über große Straßen, und oft war ein Restaurant integriert. Dies zollte der Rolle des Autos in der Nachkriegskultur Tribut: Heute würde man kaum ein Restaurant mit Blick auf endlose Blechlawinen bauen. Die Fußgängerbrücke verkörpert heute das Konzept der urbanen Freizeit und symbolisiert darüber hinaus wie alle Brücken Verbindung und Zusammenkommen. Die Vorstellung offener städtischer Räume als Erholungsräume, nicht nur als Durchgang oder Marktplatz, ist historisch nicht neu, wie Nashs Regency London oder Haussmanns Paris zeigen. Das Thema taucht immer wieder auf, es ist ein Symbol staatsbürgerlicher Reife und fördert einen entspannten Lebensstil.

Fußgängerbrücken müssen, vor allem in historischer städtebaulicher Umgebung, einen Ausgleich zwischen den Merkmalen ihres Standorts und menschlichen Maßen schaffen. Dieses Projekt, die Brücke für die EXPO 2000 in Hannover, führte über eine Straße zu den neuen Bauten der Weltausstellung. Vom Ansatz her

The pedestrian bridge has become a fin-de-siècle set-piece. From Calatrava's bridge at the Seville Expo through to Foster's Millennium Bridge in London, and new bridges in Paris, Manchester and elsewhere, there has been a vogue in the last decade for building such structures. This is not surprising if one considers the history of bridges not as being about construction but about culture. The great railway bridges of the 19th century in Britain, for example, symbolize the triumph of mercantile capitalism in the same way that the Brooklyn bridge linking Manhattan to New Jersey stands as a forerunner to the famous skyscrapers as an icon of American power.

Indeed the previous incarnation of the major pedestrian bridge, in the 1950s, took the form of the motorway bridge, often incorporating a restaurant. This is itself a tribute to the role of the car in post-war culture: few people today would site a restaurant for its views of endless traffic! What the new pedestrian bridge of today endorses is the concept of urban leisure, as well as symbolising connection and meeting, as all bridges do. The idea of urban open space as space for enjoyment, not just thoroughfare or marketplace is not historically new, witness Nash's Regency London or Haussmann's Paris. It is a recurring theme, a symbol of civic maturity, and a lifestyle of relaxation.

Pedestrian bridges need to balance the qualities of their site, especially in a historic urban context, with a human scale. This project, for a bridge on the EXPO 2000 site at Hanover, would cross a road to the new buildings of the World Fair. Its prospect could be described as forward, carrying visitors to the vision of the future on the fairground. The low sidewalls allowed the public as broad a view as possible, and the central axial fold in the walkway helped the visitor flow.

Expo 2000 Brücke: Aufsicht auf das Modell
Expo 2000 Bridge: Aerial view of model

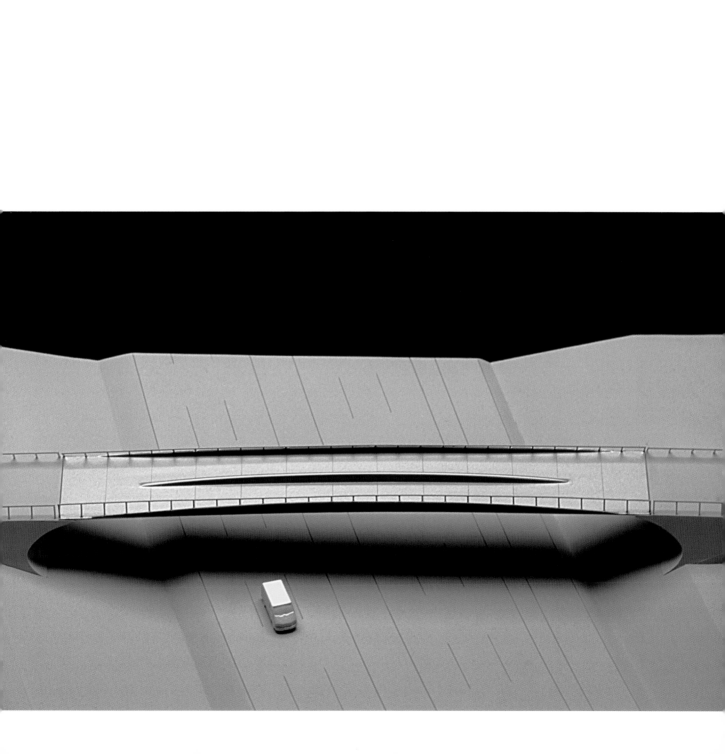

124 war sie vorwärtsgerichtet, sie trug die Besucher zu den Visionen der Zukunft auf dem Messegelände. Die niedrigen Seitenwände sorgten für die bestmögliche Aussicht, und eine in der Mitte verlaufende Falte im Gehweg teilte den Besucherstrom. Diese zentrale Überhöhung stabilisierte die Konstruktion außerdem, sodass die Seitenwände niedriger gehalten werden konnten. Die Kombination einer eleganten technischen Lösung mit einem ausdrucksstarken Designkonzept ist typisch für Werner Sobeks Arbeiten.

The central fold also provided greater structural strength, in turn allowing the side walls to be lower. The combination of an elegant technical solution with a strong design concept is typical of the works of Werner Sobek.

Das Modell von oben
Model from above

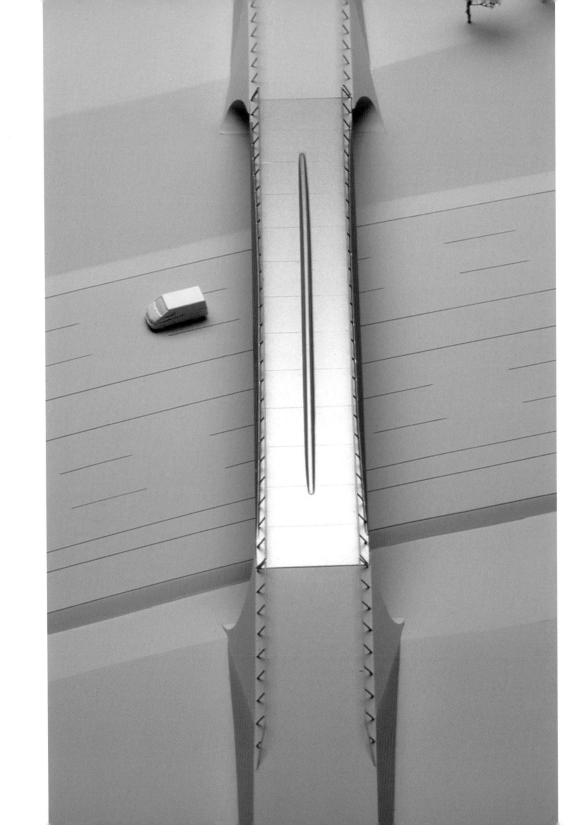

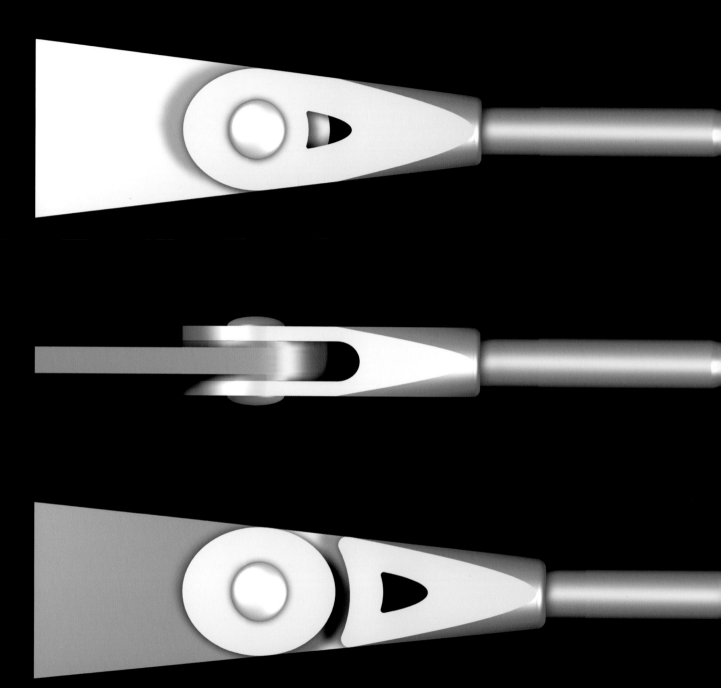

future

Eine Architektur, die den Anspruch besitzt, heute eine unserer und der kommenden Zeit angemessene Haltung zu formulieren, muss eine Architektur sein, die ihre Materialität und ihre Gestalt nicht durch Gestaltsetzung unter Rückgriff auf tradierte Formen und Materialien, sondern durch Gestaltentwicklung auf der Basis integraler Planungs- und Organisationsprozesse mit Hinblick auf aktuelle und zukünftige Formen des menschlichen Lebens findet. Die Frage lautet nicht: "Wie haben wir gewohnt und gearbeitet", sondern sie lautet: "Wie werden wir wohnen und arbeiten". Die Antwort hierauf bedingt die unbedingte Antizipation des Kommenden, ein vielleicht hie und da in die falsche Richtung führender, hinsichtlich seiner intellektuellen Vertretbarkeit aber der einzige Weg. Oder, in der Formulierung von Hegel: "... dass die Furcht zu irren schon der Irrtum selbst ist."

Eine Architektur unserer und der kommenden Zeit muss ein radikal anderes, jetzt positives Verhältnis zur natürlichen Umwelt, zu ihren Nutzern und zur ihr inhärenten Technologie haben. Die ökologische und die technologische Rückständigkeit des Bauschaffens kann nicht, trotz steter und anhaltender Versuche, aus einem Bedarf an Kontinuität oder der Legitimität des Rückgriffes auf Bewährtes in seiner tradierten Erscheinungsform insgesamt begründet werden. Es gilt stattdessen zu trennen zwischen dem, was als angemessen, bewährt, vielleicht sogar als "richtig" in einem größeren zeitlichen Rahmen bezeichnet werden kann, und seinen häufig nicht weiter hinterfragten Begleiterscheinungen.

Architecture which claims to formulate today an attitude worthy of our own and future times, should be architecture which finds its materials and forms not by dictating designs on the basis of traditional forms and materials but by developing designs and forms on the basis of integral planning and organisation processes with a view to current and future forms of human living. It is not a question of "how did we live and work?" but of "how are we going live and work in the future?". The answer requires an unconditional anticipation of what is in the offing, a path that may occasionally lead in the wrong direction but is the only possible path in terms of its intellectual justification. Or to quote Hegel: "...that the fear of erring represents error itself."

The architecture of our own and future times must exhibit a radically new and positive attitude to the natural environment, to its users and to the technology inherent in itself. The technological and ecological backwardness of building construction cannot, despite continuing attempts, be explained or justified by the necessity for continuity or by the legitimacy of having recourse to traditional practices and forms. Instead we ought to make a distinction between that which may be described as appropriate, proven or perhaps even "right" over a longer period, and its side effects which frequently are not questioned at all.

Werner Sobek

Wichtiger Bestandteil adaptiver Gebäudehüllen: Phase-Change Materials
Important element in adaptive building envelopes: phase-change materials

18

The Next Step - R 129

144 Die Literatur-Nobelpreisträgerin Toni Morrison wurde in einem Radiointerview einmal gefragt: "Warum gibt es in Ihren Romanen keine guten schwarzen Männer?" Sie antwortete mit einer Gegenfrage: "Hätten Sie Dostojewski diese Frage auch gestellt? Nein - und das zeigt doch, dass das eine sexistische und rassistische Frage ist, oder?"

Wer die Ambitionen von Ingenieuren kritisiert, gerät in die gleiche Falle. Denn diese Kritik geht oft unterschwellig davon aus, dass der Architekt qua ungeschriebenem Gesetz irgendwie "über" dem Ingenieur steht und der ambitionierte Ingenieur "sich wohl für etwas Besseres hält". Aber das Verhältnis zwischen Architekt und Ingenieur bei einem komplexen, modernen Bauprojekt zeigt, dass dieser Dualismus so anachronistisch ist, wie er klingt: Solange nicht ganz konventionell konstruiert und gebaut werden soll, muss diese Beziehung heute eine gleichberechtigte Partnerschaft sein.

Dies alles ist aber nicht nur eine Folge der Komplexität, sondern resultiert auch aus der Entwicklung unseres Verständnisses von Bauwerken als einer Struktur hin zu einem Verständnis von Bauwerken als Gesamtkomplexität, zu etwas, das funktional ist und eine eigenständige Existenz hat. (Nicht, dass diese Vorstellung bislang nicht existiert hätte, aber die Technologie zur Realisierung dieser Komplexität existierte bisher noch nicht.) Dieses Bewusstsein ist Motor und Motivation für Werner Sobeks Arbeit als Architekt und Ingenieur. Ein Gebäude ist nicht nur eine Unterkunft, sondern Teil seines sozialen, ökonomischen und physischen Umfeldes, das nicht nur Verpflichtungen schafft, sondern auch Austauschprozesse anregt.

Zum Beispiel das Projekt R 129: ein Entwurf für ein privates Wohnhaus. Der Standort spielt

The Nobel prize-winning novelist Toni Morrison was once asked in a radio interview "Why there were no good black men in her novels?" She replied with another question: "Would you have asked Dostoievsky that question? No - so what your question shows is its sexist and racist bias, isn't it!"

Those who criticize the ambitions of engineers fall into the same trap. For often their criticisms unwittingly presume that there exists some immutable hierarchy which places architects somehow "above" engineers, and that the ambitious engineer literally has "ideas above his station." A look at the relationship between architect and engineer in the context of a complex modern building project suggests that this dualism is as anachronistic as it sounds: the relationship today has to be more in the nature of a partnership, unless the construction and structural aspects are entirely conventional.

This is not just the consequence of complexity, rather of an evolution of the concept of a building from being a matter of structure to one of performance, of being something with functionality as well as existence. (Not that this perception had not existed in the past, simply that the technology to achieve it had not existed.) The work - as architect and as engineer - of Werner Sobek is empowered and motivated by this awareness. A building is not just a shelter, it is part of social, economic and physical landscapes that not only create obligations but also initiate processes of exchange.

Take the R 129 project: a concept for a private house. The site is irrelevant, since one of the guiding principles behind the design is that the structure needs no traditional foundations at all, as it can sit on a levelled piece of ground or at most be placed onto a layer of sand for stability. It will be energy efficient as far as heating and

R 129: Außenansicht
R 129: View from the exterior

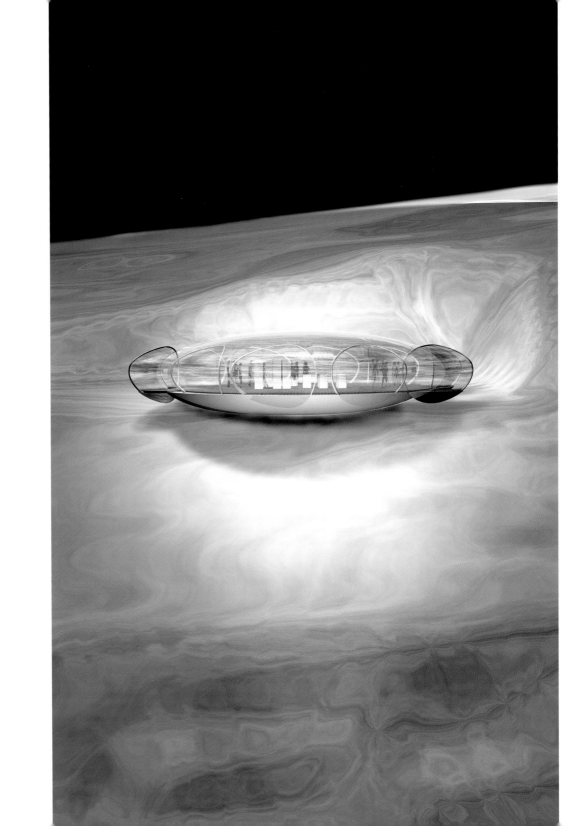

146 keine Rolle, denn eines der Leitprinzipien bei der Konstruktion war, dass der Bau kein herkömmliches Fundament braucht; er kann einfach auf einer ebenen Fläche errichtet werden, gegebenenfalls sogar nur auf einer Sandschicht. Das Haus ist in Bezug auf Heizung und Lüftung energetisch optimiert, einfach auf- und abzubauen und vollkommen rezyklierbar. Damit vereint es eine ganze Reihe von Idealvorstellungen über das perfekte Haus: es ist ein praktikables Bauwerk mit aktueller Technik.

Doch auch wenn der Entwurf nicht an einen Standort gebunden ist, darf man Letzteren nicht außer Acht lassen. Werner Sobek ist sich darüber im Klaren, dass jedes Bauwerk, wie unauffällig es auch sein mag, einen Eingriff darstellt und unterschiedliche Folgen nach sich zieht. Selbst in ländlicher Umgebung hat ein Neubau soziale Auswirkungen, er trifft eine Aussage über die Wertvorstellungen und Überzeugungen seiner Schöpfer und seiner Bewohner.

Werner Sobeks Arbeit stellt weder einen Minimalismus um seiner selbst willen noch Technik als Selbstzweck dar. Sie folgt keiner bestimmten Schule. Sobeks Arbeit wird vielmehr von einem tief empfundenen Verantwortungsbewusstsein gegenüber der Gesellschaft und der Umwelt getragen, und seiner Arbeit ist deutlich die Freude an effektiven, eleganten und harmonischen Lösungen anzumerken.

internal climate control is concerned, be simple to erect and dismantle, and be maximally recyclable. It is an ideal house only in the sense that it incorporates a number of ideas and ideals about what a house should be: it is in fact a completely feasible construction with current technology.

If the concept is not site-specific, that does not mean the site can be ignored. Werner Sobek realises that any construction, however physically tangential, is an intervention and so has consequences of different kinds. Even in a rural context a new building has social effects, it makes a statement about the values and beliefs of its creators and users.

Werner Sobek's work is neither minimalism for its own sake, nor technology for its own ends. It has no bias towards a specific agenda. Rather, Sobek's work is motivated by a deep sense of responsibility towards society and the environment, and what shines through his work is a real joy in achieving effective, elegant and harmonious solutions.

Das Innere mit anpassungsfähiger Einrichtung
Interior with adaptive furniture

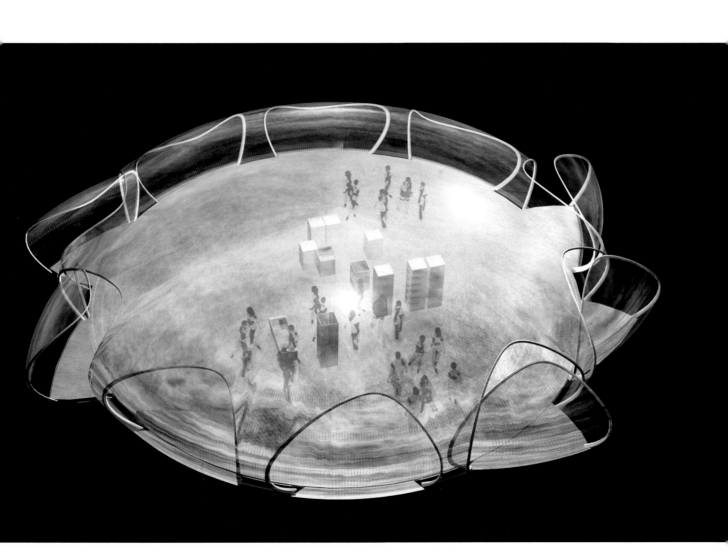

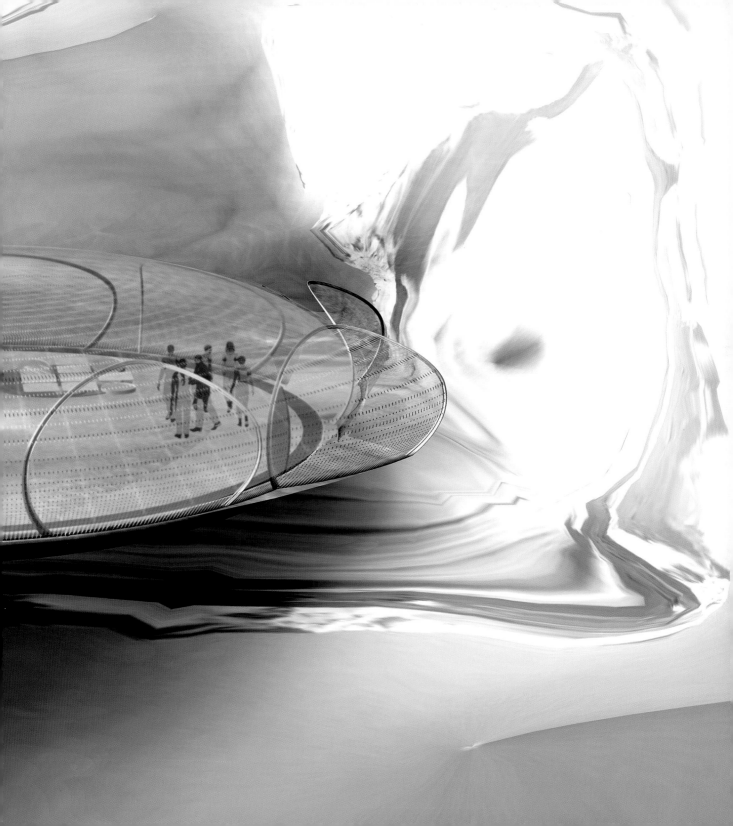

Prof. Dr. Werner Sobek

1953	geboren in Aalen, Württemberg
1974 - 1980	Bauingenieur- und Architekturstudium an der Universität Stuttgart
1980 - 1986	Wissenschaftlicher Mitarbeiter am Sonderforschungsbereich SFB 64 "Weitgespannte Flächentragwerke" an der Universität Stuttgart
1987	Promotion im Bauingenieurwesen an der Universität Stuttgart
1987 - 1991	Mitarbeiter im Ingenieurbüro Schlaich, Bergermann & Partner, Stuttgart
1991	Gründung des Ingenieurbüros Werner Sobek Ingenieure in Stuttgart Professor an der Universität Hannover (Nachfolge Bernd Tokarz) und Leiter des Instituts für Tragwerksentwurf und Bauweisenforschung
seit 1994	Professor an der Universität Stuttgart (Nachfolge Frei Otto) Direktor des Instituts für Leichte Flächentragwerke und des Zentrallabors des Konstruktiven Ingenieurbaus
seit 1998	Mitglied des Vorstands der Ingenieurkammer Baden-Württemberg Ernennung zum Prüfingenieur für Baustatik für alle Fachrichtungen
1999	Gründung des Designbüros 3e - Werner Sobek exhibition & entertainment engineering
2000	Übernahme eines zweiten Lehrstuhls als Nachfolger von Jörg Schlaich; Gründung des Instituts für Leichtbau Entwerfen und Konstruieren (ILEK) Shanghai Engineering License
2000 - 2001	Gastprofessor an der Architekturfakultät der Universität Graz
2001	Gründung von Werner Sobek Ingenieure Frankfurt Structural Engineering License für den US-Bundesstaat Illinois
2002	Mitglied der Architektenkammer Baden-Württemberg außerordentliches Mitglied des BDA Mitglied der Deutschen Akademie für Städtebau und Landesplanung
2003	Gründung des Ingenieur- und Designbüros Werner Sobek New York Peer Review Engineer in Chicago

Prof. Dr. Werner Sobek

1953	born in Aalen/Germany
1974 - 1980	studied structural engineering and architecture at the University of Stuttgart/Germany
1980 - 1986	post-graduate fellow in research project 'Wide-Span Lightweight Structures' at the University of Stuttgart/Germany
1987	PhD in structural engineering
1987 - 1991	structural engineer in the office of Schlaich, Bergermann & Partner, Stuttgart/Germany
1991 - 1994	professor at the University of Hanover/Germany (successor to Bernd Tokarz) and director of the Institute for Structural Design and Building Methods
1992	founded the engineering consultancy Werner Sobek Ingenieure in Stuttgart
since 1994	professor at the University of Stuttgart/Germany (successor to Frei Otto) director of the Institute for Lightweight Structures and of the Central Laboratory for Structural Engineering
since 1998	member of the board of the Chamber of Engineers of Baden-Württemberg proof engineer for all types of structures and materials
1999	founded the design consultancy 3e - Werner Sobek exhibition & entertainment engineering
2000	took over the chair of Jörg Schlaich; fusion of the Institute for Lightweight Structures and the Institute for Construction and Design into the Institute for Lightweight Structures and Conceptual Design Shanghai Engineering License
2000 - 2001	visiting professor at the University of Graz, Austria
2001	Structural Engineering License for the State of Illinois
2002	Architectural License for Germany honorary member of the BDA member of the German Academy for Urban Development and Environmental Planning
2003	founded the engineering and design consultancy Werner Sobek New York Peer Review Engineer in Chicago

Projektverzeichnis / Bildnachweise
Project Data / Photo credits

1. R 128 in Stuttgart (1999-2000)
Project Planning / Gesamtplanung:
Werner Sobek Ingenieure, Stuttgart
© Roland Halbe, Stuttgart

2. Deutsche Post Tower in Bonn (1997-2002)
Structural engineering / Tragwerksplanung:
Werner Sobek Ingenieure, Stuttgart
Architect / Architekt: Murphy/Jahn, Chicago
© H.G. Esch, Hennef / Zooey Braun, Stuttgart
(pp. 30-31)

3. New Bangkok International Airport
(1995-2005)
Structural engineering / Tragwerksplanung:
Werner Sobek Ingenieure, Stuttgart
Architect / Architekt: Murphy/Jahn, Chicago
© Murphy/Jahn, Chicago

4. Mercedes-Benz Exhibition Stand
Project planning / Gesamtplanung:
3e - Werner Sobek exhibition & entertainment
engineering, Stuttgart
© Andreas Keller, Altdorf

5. Rotating Umbrellas
Project planning / Gesamtplanung:
3e - Werner Sobek exhibition & entertainment
engineering, Stuttgart, mit Transsolar, Stuttgart
© 3e - Werner Sobek exhibition & entertainment engineering, Stuttgart

6. Rothenbaum Stadium (1992-1997)
Structural engineering / Tragwerksplanung:
Werner Sobek Ingenieure, Stuttgart
Architect / Architekt: Schweger & Partner,
Hamburg
© Werner Sobek Ingenieure, Stuttgart

7. Mercedes-Benz Museum (2001-2006)
Structural engineering / Tragwerksplanung:
Werner Sobek Ingenieure, Stuttgart
Architect / Architekt: UN studio, Amsterdam
© UN studio, Amsterdam (pp. 66-67) /
DaimlerChrysler AG, Stuttgart

8. Urban Street Furniture for JC Decaux (2001)
Structural engineering / Tragwerksplanung:
Werner Sobek Ingenieure, Stuttgart
Architect / Architekt: Helmut Jahn, Chicago, &
Werner Sobek, Stuttgart
© Werner Sobek Ingenieure, Stuttgart

9. Bremen University (1996-2000)
Structural engineering / Tragwerksplanung:
Werner Sobek Ingenieure, Stuttgart
Architect / Architekt: Alsop-Störmer, Hamburg
© Andreas Keller, Altdorf

10. Rhoen-Clinic in Bad Neustadt (1996-1997)
Structural engineering / Tragwerksplanung:
Werner Sobek Ingenieure, Stuttgart
Architect / Architekt: Lamm, Weber & Donath,
Stuttgart
© Werner Sobek Ingenieure, Stuttgart

11. Interbank Lima (1996-2000)
Special Structure Titanium / Sonderkonstruk-
tion Titan: Werner Sobek Ingenieure, Stuttgart
Architect / Architekt: Atelier Hollein, Wien
© Christian Richters, Münster / Werner Sobek
Ingenieure, Stuttgart (pp. 92-93)

12. MERO Exhibition Stand (2001-2002)
Project planning / Gesamtplanung:
3e – Werner Sobek exhibition & entertainment
engineering, Stuttgart
© Wolfram Janzer, Stuttgart

Zusätzliche Projekte
Additional projects

13. Audi Exhibition Stand (1998-1999)
Structural engineering / Tragwerksplanung:
Werner Sobek Ingenieure, Stuttgart
Architect / Architekt: Ingenhoven Overdiek und
Partner, Düsseldorf
© Werner Sobek Ingenieure, Stuttgart / H.G.
Esch, Hennef (pp. 110-115)

14. Airport Chair (2000-2001)
Project planning / Gesamtplanung:
3e - Werner Sobek exhibition & entertainment
engineering, Stuttgart
© Werner Sobek Ingenieure, Stuttgart /
Wolfgang Schmidberger, Stuttgart (p. 119)

15. Expo 2000 Bridge (1996-1997)
Project planning / Gesamtplanung:
Werner Sobek Ingenieure, Stuttgart
© Werner Sobek Ingenieure, Stuttgart

16. Cable Shackle (2000-2001)
Project planning / Gesamtplanung:
3e - Werner Sobek exhibition & entertainment
engineering, Stuttgart
© 3e - Werner Sobek exhibition & entertainment
engineering, Stuttgart

17. B 14 (2001)
Project planning / Gesamtplanung:
Werner Sobek Ingenieure, Stuttgart
© Werner Sobek Ingenieure, Stuttgart

18. R 129 (2001-2008)
Project planning / Gesamtplanung:
Werner Sobek Ingenieure, Stuttgart
© Werner Sobek Ingenieure, Stuttgart

Sony Center Berlin (1995-2000)
Special structures / Sonderkonstruktionen:
Werner Sobek Ingenieure, Stuttgart
Architect / Architekt: Murphy/Jahn, Chicago
© H.G. Esch, Hennef

Métafort in Paris (1995)
Conceptual design / Tragwerksentwurf:
Werner Sobek Ingenieure, Stuttgart
Architect / Architekt: LAB.F.AC., Paris
© Werner Sobek Ingenieure, Stuttgart

Kaufhof Chemnitz (1998-2001)
Structural engineering / Tragwerksplanung:
Werner Sobek Ingenieure, Stuttgart
Architect / Architekt: Murphy/Jahn, Chicago
© Roland Halbe, Stuttgart

Exhibition Stand Deutsche Post Immobilien
(2000-2001)
Project planning / Gesamtplanung:
3e - Werner Sobek exhibition & entertainment
engineering, Stuttgart
© Wolfgang Schmidberger, Stuttgart

Design Study Zeche Zollverein (2003)
Project planning / Gesamtplanung:
3e - Werner Sobek exhibition & entertainment
engineering, Stuttgart
© 3e - Werner Sobek exhibition & entertainment engineering, Stuttgart

Adaptive Building Envelopes
Ongoing research project at the Institute for
Lightweight Structures and Conceptual Design,
University of Stuttgart
© Werner Sobek Ingenieure, Stuttgart

Konzept / concept:
Werner Sobek, Conway Lloyd Morgan

Übersetzung / Translation:
Isabel Bogdan, Karl Kreuser

Gestaltung / design:
Maren Sostmann, Katerina Soukhopalov, Tilman Ockert

Texte / texts:
Conway Lloyd Morgan, Werner Sobek

Koordination, Redaktion / coordination, editing:
Frank Heinlein, Petra Kiedaisch

Korrektorat / proof reading:
Anke Beck, Vineeta Manglani

Produktion / production:
Frank Heinlein, Petra Kiedaisch

Litho, Druck / litho, print:
Leibfarth & Schwarz GmbH & Co. KG
Dettingen / Erms

Bibliographic information published by Die Deutsche Bibliothek.
Die Deutsche Bibliothek lists this publication in the Deutsche
Nationalbibliografie; detailed bibliographic data are available in
the Internet at http://ddb.de.

avedition GmbH
Verlag für Architektur und Design
Königsallee 57
D-71638 Ludwigsburg
www.avedition.de
kontakt@avedition.de

ISBN 3-89986-031-4
Printed in Germany